Bayerische Verwaltung
der staatlichen Schlösser,
Gärten und Seen

Bavarian Administration of State Castles,
Palaces, Gardens, and Lakes

Peter O. Krückmann

The Emperors, Dukes and Margraves of Franconia

From the Imperial Castle in Nuremberg to the
Residences of the Hohenzollerns and Wettins

Prestel
Munich · Berlin · London · New York

CONTENTS

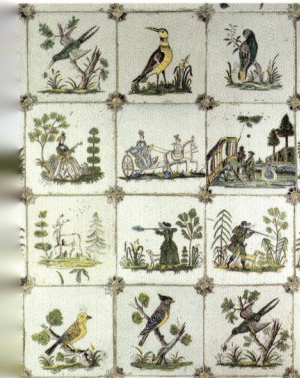

OF EMPERORS, DUKES AND MARGRAVES

In this volume, the fourth in the 'Bavaria's Castles, Palaces, Gardens and Lakes' series, the focus is on southern and eastern Franconia. In the north of this stretch of country lies the former Duchy of Coburg, which was among the possessions of the House of Wettin. In the south is an extensive tract that for centuries was ruled by the Zollerns, or 'Hohenzollerns', as they called themselves. Bordering it was the Teutonic Knights' bailiwick (*balia*) in Franconia, with Ellingen as the residential seat (*Residenz*), and the prince-bishopric of Eichstätt, two domains that, depending on the circumstances of the time, were dominated to a greater or lesser extent by the Hohenzollerns and were feuded with or courted by them. Set like an island in the middle of Zollern territory was the free imperial city of Nuremberg with its fortress of Kaiserburg, guarded and defended in early days by the Hohenzollern burgraves.

It all began in 1192 when Duke Frederick III of the Zollerns—a dynasty that could already look back on more than a century of feudal power in Swabia—became burgrave of Nuremberg, as Frederick I. Ruling a country was not the function of a burgrave (*Burggraf*, i.e. count of a *Burg* or castle), whose power resided in a castle or town, but he did carry out important administrative and political duties on behalf of his king or the Emperor. In order to strengthen their grip, which was increasingly threatened by the rise of civic power in Nuremberg, the Zollerns had by this date already acquired extensive territories in Franconia alongside their traditional possessions in Swabia. At Cadolzburg, they established a seat of their own outside the imperial city. In the mid-13th century, the towns of Bayreuth, Hof and Kulmbach fell into their hands by inheritance, culminating in 1331 with the Zollern acquisition of Ansbach. By this time, Hohenzollern Franconia represented a sizeable chunk of territory. It was therefore all too tempting to make imperial Nuremberg, located at the heart of this

The coat of arms of the Bayreuth Hohenzollerns in the Margravial Opera House.

principality, its centre. The prospect was one that filled Nuremberg's burghers with growing fear. Ever since it had been founded, their town had steadily acquired importance as an economic centre, and the presence of the Imperial Castle, the Kaiserburg, ensured that the Emperor also paid due attention to it. In 1219 Emperor Frederick II issued the city's Great Charter, which endowed it with numerous privileges and important competitive advantages. That there were irreconcilable differences between the Hohenzollern lust for territory and the burghers' desire for independence comes as no surprise. As will be seen, it was a situation that led to a war of attrition between the two parties—and which also had its comical moments.

While the Hohenzollerns were able to continue consolidating their power in Franconia outside Nuremberg, their tenure in the castle could not last.

De facto no longer masters in their part of the castle, in 1427 the discomfited burgraves finally sold it to the city of Nuremberg, after 235 years of occupation —though of course without renouncing the title (King Frederick the Great of Prussia and his successors would sport it centuries later). There was no longer any question of realizing a vision of a powerful principality of Franconia with Nuremberg as its capital. The course of history was in fact already diverted into other channels. The decision to abandon Nuremberg had been made less painful by the enfeoffment of Frederick VI as Elector of Brandenburg some ten years earlier. This allowed him to join the ranks of the most powerful German rulers of the time, and become the founder of the mighty Prussian line of Hohenzollerns.

In 1385, his father, Frederick V, had decreed that the Franconian holding should never be divided into more than two power bases. He himself divided the burgravial lands—the upland area based on Kulmbach and the lowlands based on Ansbach—between his two sons. Barely 100 years later, these two territories were reunited with the March of Brandenburg under Margrave Albert (a 'margrave' [*Markgraf*] was a count of a *Mark* or 'march', i.e. a frontier principality). One of the great German rulers of the period between the Middle Ages and the modern era, Albert was given the epithet of 'Achilles' by one of his admirers, the later pope Pius II.

The death of Margrave George Frederick in 1603 marked a turning point in the fate of Franconia. This was the year that Ansbach and Bayreuth became *Residenz* cities instead of Kulmbach, and subsequently went their separate ways for almost two centuries. They were reunited for 23 years under the last Ansbach margrave, Alexander, before being annexed by Prussia in 1791. But even this takeover was just an episode. Following a brief Napoleonic intermezzo, the territories of Ansbach and Bayreuth were finally subsumed into the Kingdom of Bavaria.

Another century would pass before the former Duchy of Coburg was to be subsumed into the Free State of Bavaria. In 1918, a referendum revealed that a clear majority of the population was in favour of being united with the Free State of Bavaria. This brought to an end over 550 years of continuous Wettin rule.

The dynastic history of the Wettins is in the meantime no less complicated than that of the Hohenzollerns in Franconia. Here, too, the family divided into separate lines, territories were extended, *Residenzen* were moved, marriages and disputes took their toll. To chronicle all that goes beyond the scope of this book, as we should have to digress to regions outside Bavaria and to the Wettin *Residenz* cities of Meissen and Dresden, Weimar and Eisenach, Gotha and Hildburghausen. Indeed, we should have to look beyond these to England and Portugal, Bulgaria and Belgium, where Wettins became princes and kings. Though Coburg was historically more oriented to the north and to the east, it has to be borne in mind that, until 1248, it was, along with Plassenburg, part of the territory of the Dukes of Merania.

Imperial Castle

Nowadays visitors can hardly discern the huge promontory that constitutes the north end of Nuremberg's old town, what with the mass of the Imperial Castle, or the Kaiserburg, built on top of it and the surrounding houses concealing the slopes. A millennium ago, it was quite different. The bluff so dominated the surrounding wooded plain that Emperor Henry III resolved to build a castle here, astride an important trade route in the heart of East Frankish territory. The purpose was twofold: to garrison imperial troops and to act as an administrative centre. Its importance—which would distinguish it from all other castles in the region—derived from its special function, to serve as the political heart of the whole empire. This was an entirely new development, for in the Middle Ages the empire had no fixed capital

It is only when you enter the castle area that you notice it is actually made up of three castles aggregated together to form a closed citadel. These days, the name Kaiserburg refers to the whole complex, but originally it designated only the western part, which is the real heart of the fortress. It is grouped around an inner bailey and protected by an outer bailey with the prominent Round Tower (Sinwellturm). East thereof is the contiguous burgravial castle with the Pentagonal Tower and St Walburga's Chapel. The outermost spur of the castle promontory is occupied by buildings of the free imperial city with the Watch Tower (Luginsland) and imperial stables. You have to know the variety of functions that the various buildings served to appreciate how the complex silhouette of the fortress came about. Moreover, owing to its long building history of around 400 years—which does not include the reconstruction work following heavy damage in the Second World War—the layout is at first glance difficult to make out. Basically three building periods have given it its present shape. The oldest part, Henry III's burgravial fort for the Salian dynasty dating from the mid-11th century, survives only as a few masonry remnants. A century or so later the Hohenstaufen emperors, in particular Barbarossa, added the

On the north side of the Imperial Castle in Nuremberg, beside the gateway, looms the massive Round Tower. Dating from the second half of the 13th century, it acted as a keep, a lookout tower and a dungeon. It signalled far and wide the power and military might of the imperial owners of the castle.

Prospect of Nuremberg from the 'Haller Book', based on Hartmann Schedel's *Nuremberg Chronicle* of 1533–36.

Kaiserburg proper, turning the purely military building into a display of imperial power. The most important Romanesque parts of the castle, the Imperial Chapel and Heathens' Tower along with parts of St Walburga's Chapel and the Pentagonal Tower, date from around 1200. The Round Tower was erected several decades later. Late Gothic additions in the 15th century changed the general look of the castle only in the detail, though the residential block (the *Palas*) and the *Kemenate* (heatable ladies' chambers) were rebuilt then and the fortifications of the imperial city were extended.

As might be expected, the most impressive part of the complex is the **Kaiserburg**, which is reached via **Heaven's Gate**. Immediately to the right looms the defiant **Round Tower**, with its Renaissance-period addition on top. In the middle of the outer bailey, protected by the Round Tower, is the **Deep Well**, which in times of siege was the only source of water. It was bored over 165 feet down into solid rock. Before going on through the second gateway into the inner bailey, one passes the **Heathens' Tower** on the left and the **Imperial Chapel**. The latter's external walls are decorated with Romanesque blind arcading and sculptures. The two vertically placed windows in the lower storey of the tower

The unmistakable silhouette of Nuremberg's Imperial Castle, whose numerous towers and variety of architectural styles reflect its chequered 400-year history.

The Romanesque Imperial Chapel in the southern part of the castle dates largely from the Hohenstaufen period. It is a double chapel, with a choir tower constructed over the sanctuary.

Right: View through the nave to the choir of the lower chapel.

The slender, light-coloured columns with their almost classical-looking capitals reflect the imperial use of the light-filled upper chapel, compared with the rather squat lower chapel.

View from the lower chapel through the opening to the groin vaulting in the upper chapel.

The noted eagle capital with its typically Romanesque figurative decoration.

admit light to the two chancels of the Imperial Chapel, which is a double chapel.

Whereas the two chancels, one on top of the other, form part of the Heathens' Tower, the rest of the chapel is absorbed into the adjacent building. The different styles of the doors to the two chapels indicate that they served different purposes. The lower chapel was accessible from the outside by a side doorway to those who were not residents of the *Palas*. The upper chapel, on the other hand, can be entered only from the Knights' Hall of the *Palas*, and the galleries there led directly into the imperial apartments. This arrangement reflects the hierarchy of the late medieval ruling class with its three levels: the ministerials (household officers), the royal household and the emperor.

Naturally, the architecture of the chapels likewise corresponds to their functions. The lower chapel is virtually square, divided by four columns into three bays and three aisles. The groin-vaulted space appears heavy and gloomy. Romanesque ornamentation is found mainly on the capitals, notably the celebrated eagle capital. The structural sturdiness is in part dictated by the needs of statics, of course, but the great contrast with the upper chapel shows that architectural necessity can also indicate differences of rank. Though built to the same ground plan, the upper chapel is lofty, light-filled. It is almost devoid of Romanesque character, taking on well-nigh Gothic proportions. In contrast to the dark sandstone of the lower chapel, a light, marble-like limestone was used for the slender columns.

Late Gothic doorway in the Knights' Hall. Christ the judge is enthroned at the apex, flanked by the Virgin and St John the Baptist. Below kneel Emperor Frederick III (1415–1493), on the left, and his son Maximilian I (1459–1519), on the right.

The galilee bay of the upper chapel is divided into two storeys. The lower part provides access to the chapel, while the upper storey forms the imperial gallery. The latter is not especially ornate, except for a small oratory built into a wall of the south bay in 1520. Painted on its walls are tendrils and scenes from Albrecht Dürer's *Life of the Virgin.* The oratory was warmer than the rest of the chapel in the cold winter months, but it also served to set the emperor apart from the rest of the congregation. The upper and lower chapels are linked via an opening in the centre bay, so that mass could be celebrated jointly despite the spatial separation. Christianity could thus be viewed as the bond that links all social classes.

The two largest rooms in the castle are the Knights' Hall (left) and the Imperial Hall (right) above it.

West of the chapel is the **Palas**. With its two spacious halls and adjacent rooms, this served both a public function and as a private residence for the emperor. The lower storey contains the **Knights' Hall**, which is impressive for its timbered ceiling carried on 30 transverse beams supported by five oak columns. Here the emperor dined in state. A fine late Gothic doorway connects the hall with the upper chapel, while a staircase leads to the **Imperial Hall** above. Formerly furnished with tables and sideboards, it was the scene of festive banquets.

The south-west door leads from the hall into the three **imperial chambers**. Substantial parts of the wall coverings were saved before the wartime destruction of the castle, so that these rooms can once again be presented in largely their original form. The first room, the **Reception Room**, is notable for its armorial ceiling. Numerous coats-of-arms of the Austro-Spanish empire greet the visitor's gaze, emphasizing the greatness and power of Emperor Charles V. In the following room, the striking feature is the ceiling with the huge double-headed imperial eagle, which survives from the work commissioned by Frederick III in the late 15th century. The last room is the Corner Chamber. As in the previous two rooms, there is an imposing tiled stove here. This masterpiece of the Nuremberg Renaissance around 1550 was presumably designed by the renowned Nuremberg-based artist Peter Flötner.

The imperial Reception Room with its ornate armorial ceiling, which was probably painted by Albrecht Dürer's pupil Hans Springinklee in 1520.

Below: Double-headed imperial eagle, from a 15th-century ceiling painting in the Imperial Chamber.

This 17th-century, art-historically important tiled stove in the imperial chambers was the work of Nuremberg artists Johann Vest and Georg Vest III.

The architectural combination of the *Palas* as the public statement of state power and the Imperial Chapel as an emblematic building of a religiously based and integrated ruling hierarchy has produced a building complex of great symbolic force. The Kaiserburg in Nuremberg thus became a model for European absolutist architecture of whatever style right up to the Rococo period.

In the face of such systematic iconography hammering home imperial might, it is hardly surprising that the area of the **burgravial castle** is much less impressive. The main job of the burgraves was to guard and administer the castle—even though this was where the Hohenzollerns first nourished ambitions for a territorial base of their own. What the actual burgravial castle looked like we no longer know. Until it was destroyed in fighting in 1420, it occupied the area in the north between the **Vestnertor** gateway and the **Pentagonal Tower**, comprising two fortified areas of key importance. The walls of the Pentagonal Tower are over eight feet thick. South of this is **St. Walburga's Chapel**. Following repeated fires and reconstruction, only the lower part of the tower now dates from the Romanesque period.

The **free imperial city buildings** occupy the eastern part of the castle hill. They, too, are dominated by a tower, the **Luginsland**. Built in a mere 40 days in 1377, it was intended to protect the city from encroachment by the Hohenzollerns and afford a view of what was going on in the burgravial castle. The tower was thus a visible sign of the growing conflict

Heaven's Stables (right) and adjacent Hasenburg and Heaven's Gate, which opened directly onto the town. It was breached in the older city wall in 1377, when tensions between emperor and burgrave ran high.

between the two adversaries. Its presence prompted Burgrave Frederick V to complain to the emperor—though without effect—that he was no longer master in his own castle.

In 1422, only two years after the destruction of the burgravial castle, the office of castellan charged with looking after the Imperial Castle was transferred to the city of Nuremberg, indicating that the Hohenzollerns had finally lost their power base on the castle rock for good. In 1427, they therefore sold the area to the city, which 70 years later erected the huge **imperial stables** between the Pentagonal Tower and Luginsland, again in the remarkably short time of exactly one year. Despite the name, the principal function of the building was as a grain store, which accounts for the steep roof with six storage lofts. Only in the 16th century was the building used as stalls for the imperial horses, during meetings of the Imperial Diet.

Stone carving of the city arms on the imperial stables, 1494/95, by Nuremberg sculptor Adam Kraft.

Top left: Nuremberg's Imperial Castle seen from the north. From left to right: Luginsland, the imperial stables, Pentagonal Tower, Round Tower and castellan's residence. Water-coloured drawing, *c.* 1530.

The Pentagonal Tower, erected in the second half of the 12th century, is one of the few surviving parts of the burgravial castle. The imperial 'stables' in the background were in fact built and long used as a granary.

Katharina Tucher and Lorenz II, the
builders of Tucher Palace, painted by
Hans Schäufelein in 1534.

ICON PVDICAE INVIOLATAEQ: FIDEI MATRONAE CATERINAE STRAVBIAE LAVRENTII
DVCHERI CONIVGIS GERMANAE ANNO AETATIS SVAE TRICES TERTIO

ICON OPT VIRI EXPATRICIO ORDINE CLARI LAVRENTII TVCHERI MARTINI FILII
NORIBERGENSIS ANNO AETATIS SVAE QVADRAGES TERT

Tucher Palace

Once the Kaiserburg was built, a settlement grew up at the foot of the hill,
where castle folk, artisans and merchants resided. The settlement expanded
extremely quickly and soon had a social structure of its own, independently of
the castle. Before long, at the head of the population, there was (from 1256
onwards) a patriciate that governed the city, consisting of the most influential
families. The close links maintained between the city and the imperial house
led to the granting of numerous privileges, establishing a basis for Nuremberg
to develop into one of the most powerful trading cities of Europe in the
Middle Ages.

The free imperial city of Nuremberg eventually acquired extensive tracts
of land outside its own walls, where the prosperous upper crust of Nuremberg built country houses in which to spend the summer months. Yet, even
within the three-mile girth of the city walls, there were estates with a rural
character, but enough visible self-assurance to proclaim the wealth and pride of
their patrician owners. One such building was the Tucher Palace, set in its own
grounds. It was constructed between 1533 and 1544 by the mercantile widely
ramified Tucher family, to a design that was supplied by architect Paulus
Beheim.

In contrast to the showy character of court architecture, which is in
general equally manifest within and without, the street front of the three-storey
house is plain and self-contained. Only a small oriel—a so-called Nuremberg
Chörlein—adorns the irregular façade. On the front facing the delightful courtyard and garden there is a quirky staircase tower with more elaborate decorations. In accordance with traditional Nuremberg practice, the two-wing entrance
vestibule still has a late Gothic reticulated vault, while the residential rooms
and hall in the upper floors manifest Renaissance trappings.

Except for the stair tower and external walls, the house was destroyed
during an air raid in the final months of the Second World War. After it was
reconstructed, the city of Nuremberg installed a museum in it that affords a
glimpse into the world of the Nuremberg patriciate.

Cadolzburg Castle seen from the west. Visible here are the massive outer walls and the Old Building with the adjacent chapel.

Cadolzburg Castle, near Fürth

Long before they withdrew from the imperial city, the Zollern burgraves were well aware that, owing to the constant disputes with the burghers of Nuremberg, the city could never be the centre of their principality in Franconia. Some 15 miles west of Nuremberg they therefore erected a new castle known as Cadolzburg. Here, in a territory they already firmly controlled, they could go about their business without confrontation, setting up a second centre of power alongside Plassenburg Castle in Kulmbach.

Cadolzburg's building history goes back to the mid-13th century, when the Hohenzollerns had acquired control of the castle's predecessor. Since then, the castle has had a chequered history. It was continually extended until Margrave Albert Achilles moved the residency to Ansbach in 1456. Thereafter it served as a secondary *Residenz*, especially in the summer months. Time and again, it became involved in military conflicts, but the damage it sustained was never as great as in April 1945, when it was completely gutted in a fire. Since 1982, the Bavarian Administration of Castle and Palaces has been reconstructing it at great expense.

Being constantly under threat from the Nuremberg burghers, massive fortifications were necessary. The first step was to enclose the small settlement outside the gates of the castle within walls. After passing through the outer gate, you enter the outer bailey, a spacious terrain enclosed by working buildings. Those there now date largely from the 18th and 19th centuries. The fortress proper is reached via a second gate, above which the huge keep rises, the symbol and best-protected part of the stronghold. The eye is first drawn to the Gothic chapel wing, which subdivides the inner bailey and abuts the **Old Building** from the mid-15th century. With its ornate oriels and stellar-vaulted hall, it was intended to satisfy its powerful owners' need for princely display. The subsequent **New Building** erected opposite evolved from the medieval *Palas*. Renaissance gables and large windows give Cadolzburg Castle the appearance of a palace.

Cadolzburg Castle, painted by Georg Anton Graef c. 1870.

Plassenburg Castle

One of the proudest fortresses in the German empire was Plassenburg Castle, situated on a hill overlooking the town of Kulmbach. Its history goes back to the mid-13th century, when Otto VIII of the Meranian dynasty built a castle here. After Otto died, the Thuringian Counts of Orlamünde became lords of Plassenburg Castle for almost a century. A succession agreement finally left possession with the Hohernzollerns under Frederick V. The present appearance of the castle dates back to the period after 1554, when it was splendidly rebuilt following major war damage, inducing its architect, Caspar Vischer, to boast in 1573: 'There is no fortress like it in Germany'.

Vischer was one of the greatest German architects of the Renaissance, who was also involved in the construction of Heidelberg Castle. Plassenburg Castle, for which he took responsibility in 1562, is rectangular, arranged round a courtyard, which, owing to its elegant design, is called the Beautiful Courtyard. The arcading with its extensive sculptural work opens as an impressive sandstone showpiece towards the court, on the model of northern Italian *castelli* of the period, wholly in contrast with the defiant look of the castle's exterior. This mixture of military strength and stately splendour has been interpreted as an expres-

The so-called Beautiful Courtyard in the east wing of Plassenburg Castle, whose two-storey arcading is based on Italian models.

A room in the margravial apartments with Margravine Maria's octagonal state bed. Made around 1630, it is Plassenburg's sole surviving original piece of furniture.

sion of the double function of Plassenburg as both protective fortress and grand residence.

From an architectural point of view the most ambitious rooms in the stronghold are the Margrave's Apartments on the first floor. All the rooms are provided with post-Gothic vaulting supported by short, sturdy half-columns. Otherwise somewhat plain, the rooms were kept warm by fine Renaissance-style fireplaces.

Beside the showpiece rooms, the castle also accommodates several museums today, including the Upper Main Landscape Museum and German Pewter Figures Museum, the Army Museum of Frederick the Great and the Margravial Museum, which is devoted to the Hohenzollerns in Franconia.

View of the castle chapel with its lateral galleries.

Lauenstein Castle

With its slate roof typical of the region, Lauenstein Castle can be seen for miles. Getting there is somewhat more complicated. It bestrides a craggy spur, dominating the little town of Ludwigsstadt and its surrounding wooded countryside. Entering the west gate from the town, one immediately notices the Brandenburg eagle on the keystone and the inscription 'F.M.Z.B.C.' along with the date 1749—'Frederick, Margrave of Brandenburg-Culmbach', of whom we shall hear much more below. By this time, the castle already looked back on a long history of over six centuries. Being in an exposed position in the northern marches of Franconia, the castle was of great strategic and administrative importance for all the rulers who resided here from the 12th century onwards, from the Counts of Merania via the Counts of Orlamünde to the Hohenzollerns, who acquired the feudal overlordship of the castle under Margrave Frederick of Brandenburg in 1427. This is reflected in the degree of fortification of the stronghold.

From the gatehouse one must cross a moat to reach the enclosed **outer bailey**. The oldest part, the 12th-century former keep, is now recognizable only from the foundation walls to the right. Beside it looms the **Orlamünde Building**, largely dating from the 14th century but thoroughly 'improved' in the Renais-

South-west corner of the inner courtyard of Lauenstein Castle, showing the Thüna Building (left) and the Orlamünde Building (right).

Right: Lauenstein Castle seen from the west.

Stained-glass window depicting Otto of Orlamünde.

The Prayer Room in the Thüna Building, whose name derives from the 16th-century picture cycle depicting the Passion, parts of which are still original.

sance style in the second half of the 16th century under the lords of Thüna. They were also responsible for the construction of the **main building** of the same name in the north-east of the courtyard.

In 1791 the castle fell into Prussian hands before being incorporated into Bavaria 12 years later. By then it served no useful purpose, and abandonment and ruin seemed its likely fate. However, in 1896 it was acquired by a private citizen, Ehrhard Messmer, who embarked on a thorough programme of restoration inspired by historicism and Art Nouveau. Finally, in 1962, Lauenstein and its extensive historic collections passed into the hands of the Bavarian Castles Administration.

The two-aisle Orlamünde Hall occupies virtually the whole ground floor of the Orlamünde Building.

BAYREUTH

Margravine Wilhelmina of Bayreuth (1709–1758), painted by Antoine Pesne c. 1734. New Palace, Bayreuth.

After Bayreuth was founded by the Counts of Andechs-Merania, scarcely more than half a century elapsed before the ambitious Hohenzollerns, who had just been made burgraves of Nuremberg, took over the town, in 1194. There they remained in control until 1806, i.e. for more than 600 years. However, it did not become a *Residenz* until 1603, when Cölln an der Spree(i.e. Berlin)-born Christian of the cadet branch of Hohenzollerns came to power following the extinction of the elder line. Soon thereafter the young margrave initiated the ambitious project of rebuilding the medieval castle. The most striking feature of the ornamentation is the array of sculptural busts of classical gods, emperors and contemporary rulers recalling Plassenburg Castle in Kulmbach, where similar adornments bore witness to the high status of the castle as a margravial *Residenz*.

However, Bayreuth's golden age came 130 years later, when Margrave Frederick and his consort, Wilhelmina, came into the title. Under them, the town acquired its now familiar splendour, with the Margravial Opera House and the New Palace, in addition to numerous Baroque townhouses and grand new avenues. The Hermitage just outside the town was extended and Sanspareil Park, between Bayreuth and Bamberg, was completely redesigned.

All this building activity gave rise to a townscape whose ostentation and wealth can only be interpreted as an expression of pride in the margravial couple's family connections. Both Frederick and Wilhelmina were members of the Brandenburg Hohenzollern dynasty. Wilhelmina was the daughter of 'Soldier King' Frederick William and sister of Frederick the Great, i.e. of the Berlin branch, while Frederick came from the Franconian side. The couple held sway for 30 years, during which time the finances of the margravate went totally to pot, but Bayreuth became a byword for 18th-century German art and culture.

Garden front of the Hermitage, later called the Old Palace.

HERMITAGE

Following chronology, we start our tour of the Bayreuth of Margravine Wilhelmina at the Hermitage. Located a few miles outside town, the Hermitage is a country house, later renamed the **Old Palace**. It overlooks extensive wooded grounds on the slopes of the Red Main River valley. The house and park were laid out in 1715 by Margrave George William, an uncle of Margrave Frederick. In 1735, the year he succeeded to the title, Frederick gave the Hermitage to his wife, whereupon Wilhelmina immediately set to work extending the small house, turning it into a Rococo jewel. It is so very much her own work that visiting the Old Palace, particularly the Ladies' Wing, is not only a revelation of unique interior furnishings, but also a reflection of its creator's frame of mind and personal tastes.

Visitors enter the house from the park via the well-preserved central **Marble** or **Great Hall**. George William had dedicated the room to the Red Eagle Order he had founded, and the decorative scheme alludes to this. From here, one enters the **Antechamber** of the **Margravine's Wing**. The ceiling painting by Wilhelm Ernst Wunder is very revealing. It shows Roman women who—following an account by Roman historian Livy—saved their city from sacking by handing over their money and jewellery to the enemy. This history painting sets the scene for a series of self-allegorizations continued in the following rooms.

The ceiling fresco in the Great Hall, painted by Gabriel Schreyer for Margrave George William, depicts the Greek god Apollo as an allegory of an absolutist monarch.

Here it is a model of virtuous behaviour. Just as the women sacrificed their goods and chattels for the benefit of the state, so would Wilhelmina as a good ruler place the welfare of the state above her own interests.

Next is the **Audience Chamber**, whose special status is marked by more opulent decoration. An interesting feature is the painted ceiling signed 'Stephanus Torelli Pinxit Anno 1740' and illustrating the unfamiliar story of Cheilonis and Cleombrotus. The latter was banished by his father-in-law, the Spartan king Leonidas II, after usurping his throne, and his wife, Cheilonis, followed him into exile. This is a most remarkable episode to show in an audience chamber. Various clues—for example, Wilhelmina's dog Folichon is sitting at Cheilonis's feet—indicate that here again the margravine was referring to herself. She, too, had been sent away by her parents, to Bayreuth to be married. Her memoirs suggest that Wilhelmina very much took this as banishment, but that at the same time she accepted her destiny with an attitude that matched the regal dignity of her brother, i.e. as a servant of the state. Once again, this is an example of virtuous behaviour, which is why the unusual exile scene is in a prominent position in the Audience Chamber.

Wilhelmina was, however, not the sort of person to accept such a situation as a hopeless fate. In fact, the opposite is the case, because the margravine set herself the task of turning her court in Bayreuth into an earthly paradise. This is presented in the subsequent **Japanese Room**. Here the drama of the Audience Chamber gives way to Far Eastern serenity. The walls are covered with lacquered paintings depicting all facets of a happy life at a royal Chinese court—or at least as life there was imagined in Europe. Enthroned above it in stucco on the ceiling is the wise, smiling figure of Wilhelmina with Chinese features as the patroness of such earthly bliss.

Ever since classical times, music has been considered a symbol of divine and cosmic harmony. Composed according to the laws of harmony, it was supposed to calm the souls of players and audience alike, bring them into harmony and transport them into a higher sphere. That a musical nature leads to the highest form of human coexistence and true friendship among human beings is illustrated in the **Music Room**. The stuccowork of the ceiling shows Orpheus,

Far Eastern cheerfulness and intimacy radiate from the Japanese Room adjacent to the Audience Chamber, the latter tending to be reserved for official business. Two of the lacquered panels (right) were a present from Frederick the Great, the margravine's brother.

Central in the ceiling stuccowork of the Music Room is Orpheus, who could even move animals with his song.

Wilhelmina's Music Room, the décor of which dates from 1745.

whose voice and strings could move not only humans but also animals and even plants and trees. Below, painted female portraits set into the walls show women close to the margravine, who established a circle of friends here.

A further ornate room is the **Chinese Mirror Room**, which Wilhelmina was particularly fond of. Being apart from the actual public areas, it was perhaps the most intimate room in the whole house. Seven years after it was built, the room was refurnished. The most important change was the insertion of irregularly cut mirrors of varying sizes covering the walls in random order. This eccentric feature—quite contrary to conventional European tastes of the day—gave rise to numerous romantic interpretations, the most common of which is 'shattered dreams and

The unusual Chinese Mirror Room, from c. 1750, was Wilhelmina's private study, where she wrote her memoirs.

Margravine Wilhelmina, painted by Jean-Etienne Liotard in 1745.

distorted reality'. In fact, the irregularly shaped mirrors are a metaphor for nature—nature as a counterfoil to a strictly ordered court life.

To recapitulate the sequence of the principal rooms in the Margravine's Wing: the Antechamber celebrates virtue, which expresses willingness to make sacrifices for the state. The motif of sacrifice reappears in the subsequent Audience Chamber in more dramatic form. Wilhelmina sacrifices herself by going into exile with her husband. Prompted by Chinese philosophy, she transforms the Franconian *Residenz*, her place of exile, into an idealized Asiatic court, which is illustrated in the Japanese Room. The Music Room could be described as a sanctuary of heavenly peace. Even opposing and predatory emotions can be reconciled by Orpheus's music. Finally, the Mirror Room is the place of spiritual contemplation and solitary meditation, dedicated literally and metaphorically to reflection. Here the individual reaches his/her goal on the path from the outer to the inner world.

From this cloister-like setting, wholly secluded from the outside world, a staircase leads to the lower-lying **grotto**, in the rear of the building. It rises several storeys high, and is decorated with glass shards and shells up to the lantern of the dome. Like the Marble Hall, it dates back to the very first building period, as the monogram of George William over the door indicates. Later, Wilhelmina and Frederick also had their initials added. Along with numerous dolphins,

The ceiling frescoes of the Antechamber and Audience Chamber were painted by Bayreuth court painter Wilhelm Ernst Wunder. In them, Margrave Frederick is identified with celebrated classical commanders Themistocles and Alexander the Great.

One of the fabulous shell creatures in the Grotto, which is part of the original building work at the Old Palace commissioned by Margrave George William.

grotesques and imaginary creatures, the principal delights are the fountains. Even though the grotto may no longer have all 200 spouts of yore, it pays to check carefully where you stand during a demonstration!

In the **Margrave's Wing** in the west, the way leads past simple hermits' cells from the first building period until you reach the ruler's **Bedroom**. An original feature here is the rather saucy plaster relief over the fireplace. It shows a naked putto, presumably Cupid, holding up the locket of a virtually unclad beauty, i.e. Venus. The ceiling of the next room but one, the **Antechamber**, is also adorned with elegant stuccowork, dating from around 1750. Frothy Rococo ornamentation depicting fountains, plants and fish evokes a bizarre garden and alludes to the park at the Hermitage.

The most splendid room in this wing of the building is of course the **Audience Chamber**. The gilt carvings with military emblems indicate that this room is intended to convey state power. The ceiling painting by Bayreuth court painter Wilhelm Ernst Wunder shows the Persian king Artaxerxes receiving the successful Athenian general Themistocles after the latter had been banished from his native city by his fellow citizens. As in the corresponding room on the margravine's side, the painting alludes to the real-life story of the margravial couple in the form of an exile scene.

The last room on the tour is another **Antechamber**, where the ceiling shows the young Alexander being reprimanded by Leonidas for throwing too much incense into the sacrificial fire. Together with the original wall hangings, the theme of which is the heroic deeds of Alexander the Great, the overall conceit here is that even as heir Frederick already possessed the ruler's virtue of magnanimity, and after taking power had proved himself a great ruler, comparable only with Alexander.

Following this perambulation through the Old Palace, exploring the backdrop of symbolism employed by Wilhelmina and her husband, it is time to move on to the other structures at the Hermitage that the margravine went on to construct until her death.

No less unusual is the **New Palace**, with which Wilhelmina created a further highlight of the Hermitage. Around 1750, west of the already existing

house, which has since then been called the Old Palace, she created some fascinating park architecture. The focus of the oval layout is the **Sun Temple**, from which two tracts of arcading extend to form a semicircle. These served as winter gardens for exotic plants, and they used to have large aviaries at the ends. Towards the north, the area was enclosed in an oval by trellises (now partly reconstructed) with sandstone vases placed among them.

Again, the sense of the design requires symbolic interpretation. The Sun Temple represents the palace of the sun god Apollo in the firmament, which the latter leaves every morning with his chariot (as mythology has it) in order to cross the world during the day and illuminate it with his light. The world below him is suggested by the oval of the rest of the design. The water basin stands for the sea, the aviaries with the birds in them for the air and the display of plants for the earth. The decoration with red, blue and yellow rivers of glass and rock crystals, which lend the Sun Temple and the two wing structures an enchanting appearance, fit nicely into this interpretation, since Apollo's palace was made of crystal. Naturally the whole building served to glorify Margrave Frederick as a Brandenburg Apollo ruling over the seasons and bringing life to the margraviate of Bayreuth with the rays of his wisdom and greatness. Unfortunately nothing survives of the unusual interiors because of bomb damage in the Second World War.

The New Palace at the Hermitage, with the Sun Temple, which is graced with orangeries on each side.

The dome of the Sun Temple with putti pointing to the sky. The centre is a sun-wheel formed of rocailles and other Rococo ornaments.

27

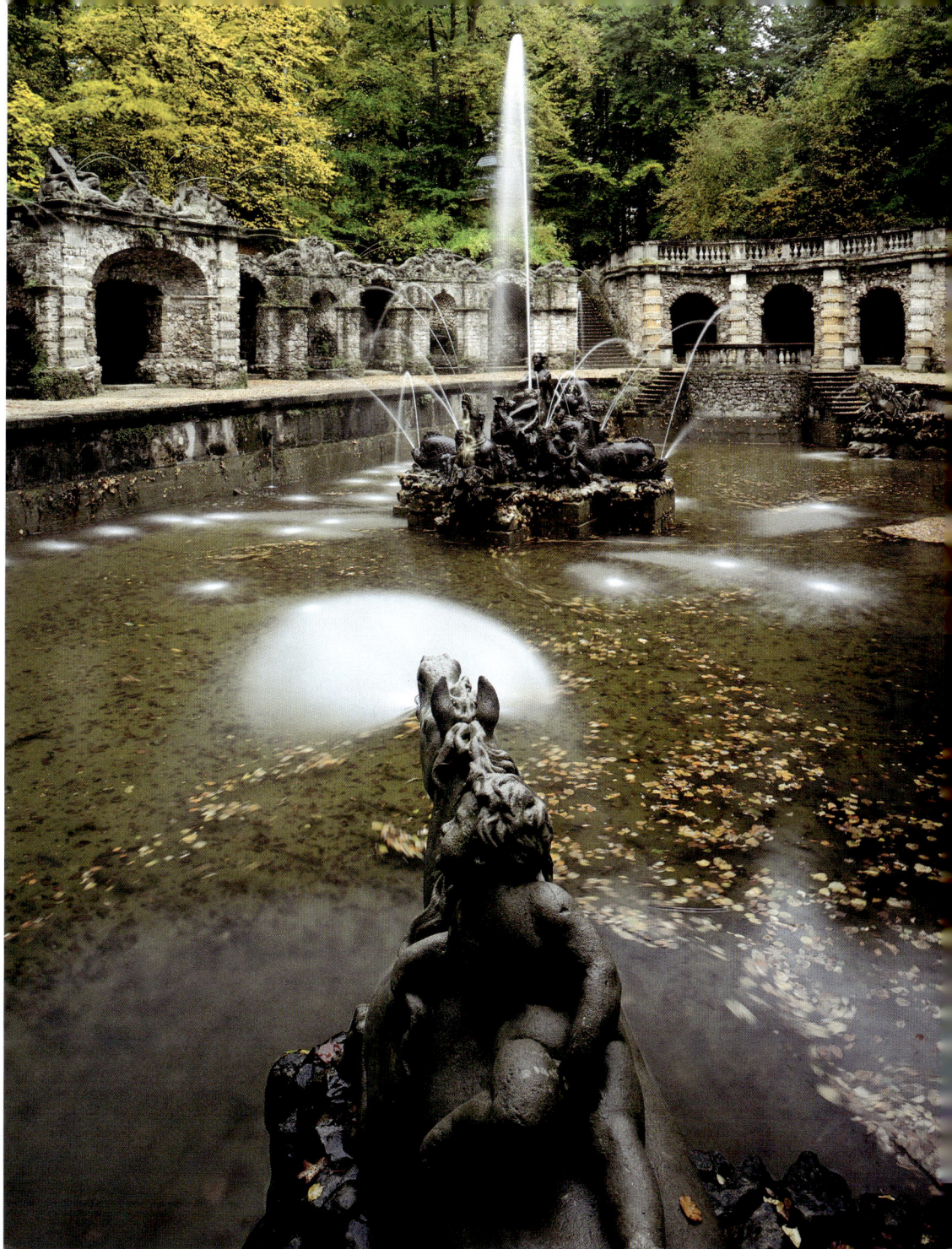

Looking north towards the pool through the open French windows of the Sun Temple.

The Lower Grotto is in a secluded part of the woods in the Hermitage park.

The Ruined Theatre in the Hermitage park was built by Joseph Saint-Pierre in 1743–45.

When walking round the **park**, don't fail to visit the **Ruined Theatre** near the Old Palace, which Margravine Wilhelmina had built in 1743/44 for the performance of minor operas and comedies.

No less impressive is the **Lower Grotto** dating from 1745, whose fountains survive in their entirety. It consists of a pool graced with a lively sculptural group of nymphs and sea-horses. Towards the slope it is enclosed by classical grotto architecture. A relatively small structure on the eastern side served as a *maison de plaisance* for the margrave, and even had a bath installed on the ground floor.

Not far from here is a plain residential building occupied by Wilhelmina while reconstruction work was being carried out on the Old Palace. She christened this little house **Monplaisir** (denoting 'my pleasure' in French)—a name that would become programmatic for the whole Hermitage ensemble under the margravial couple Frederick and Wilhelmina.

29

MARGRAVIAL OPERA HOUSE

'The last day or two I've been looking at the new opera house. I was very pleased with it. The interior is almost complete. In this theatre, Bibiena has united the quintessence of the Italian and French styles. One must admit that he is an unsurpassed master in his profession.' These lines, written on 14 May 1748 by Margravine Wilhelmina to her brother Frederick the Great in Brandenburg, only hint at the extent to which Wilhelmina must actually have been impressed by the almost complete opera house.

The pride of the margravine is understandable if we remember the circumstances under which building commenced. A magnificent opera house was to be built in the small *Residenz* town of a minor German principality far from European centres and trade routes—this was the ambition that Wilhelmina and her husband, Frederick, had nurtured. They turned the dream into reality over the extraordinarily brief construction period of four years.

Back in 1743, existing performance venues had been found so inadequate and so unworthy of the margravate that in November Wilhelmina wrote to her brother in Berlin requesting the plans for his Unter den Linden opera house, which court architect Georg Wenzeslaus von Knobelsdorff had just completed. In the end, Wilhelmina opted for a different approach, and commissioned Bayreuth court architect Joseph Saint-Pierre to erect the building and its austere façade and Giuseppe Galli Bibiena (the most famous theatre architect of the

Unlike the façade, the auditorium was built in the opulent style of the Italian Baroque. The marriage celebrations of Frederick and Wilhelmina's only daughter, Frederica Sophia (1732–1780), were held here in 1748.

The austere French Baroque façade of the Opera House bears a closer resemblance to that of a palace than a theatre.

day) and his son Carlo to execute the interior. The interior is in the heavy Italian Baroque style typical of these inspired theatre architects, and is quite different from light-hearted Bayreuth Rococo.

As with the Old Palace at the Hermitage, the architectural and decorative structure of the opera house becomes evident only if you walk through it as the margravial couple would once have done for a performance.

The Neoclassical façade, with its pillared portico in the style of a classical temple, provides a duly majestic reception. A fanfare of trumpets and drums from the balcony would once have greeted the princely couple. With unfulfilled expectations of a correspondingly splendid interior, visitors pass initially into a low, plain vestibule. The foyer is reached from this. And what a contrast! Unlike the vestibule, the foyer occupies no less than three storeys. On entering it, one gets a sense of space, and instinctively straightens up. To each side are three

View of the auditorium from the stage. It has three tiers of seating, in addition to the ornate Prince's Box in the centre. The ceiling painting depicts the arrival of Apollo and the muses.

Allegories of princely majesty with sceptre and crown, and Prudence, seated in the left-hand herald's box, holding her attribute, a mirror with a snake.

A putto on the Prince's Box.

ranks of balustrades, effectively spectator galleries where everyone could watch the princely couple entering as if they, too, were on stage. This is not, of course, the auditorium itself. That is reached by a strangely narrow, plain dark passage. In passing through it and entering the auditorium, one is admitted to a realm in which poetry is lent visual form. Completely shut off from the real world, you are presented with the reality of an artistic world.

Everything here is both real and unreal. When the stage was decorated, it and the auditorium united to form an infinitely spacious ruler's palace. Angels and putti float through the air, animated faces look at us out of the decoration and the ceiling opens up to reveal a glimpse of Apollo and his retinue in the painting there. They have just reached a cloud, to establish a new homeland in margravial Bayreuth.

An event that prompted the building of the opera house was the engagement of Duke Charles Eugene of Württemberg to Wilhelmina and Frederick's only child, Elizabeth Frederica Sophia, who was just 12 at the time. The building was sufficiently advanced four years later for it to open with performances and a banquet to celebrate the marriage.

Sanspareil Rock Garden and Zwernitz Castle

It was not only the Margravial Opera House that was commissioned around the same time by Wilhelmina and Frederick. Another innovation was a small but highly unusual landscape garden some distance from Bayreuth, halfway to Bamberg. The region had always been famous for its strange tuff formations, which supposedly prompted one guest to exclaim: 'C'est sans pareil!' (It's incomparable.) Wilhelmina herself was so taken with this natural phenomenon that from 1744, once her daughter's marriage was contracted, a park was laid out at her behest to mark the occasion. Many of the rocks had Chinese pavilions and rustic cabins built on them, and the 'ruined' rock theatre is particularly impressive.

A small hermitage was also constructed. It consisted of the **Oriental Building**, two houses and a kitchen facility. Owing to rebuilding in the 19th century, it is no longer evident that the main building, the Oriental Building, was originally a little Chinese temple with pagoda roofs. Of the rooms, the domed principal room is especially notable. This opens into two lateral wings and a picturesque inner courtyard. As far as the garden is concerned, it was not the enjoyment of nature that excited Wilhelmina primarily but the supposed Chinese look of the rocks. Asymmetrical and fissured, pierced by holes and vistas, they are reminiscent of illustrations in travel books about China in Wilhelmina's library.

The not very large but well-preserved **Zwernitz Castle** in the immediate vicinity provides a charming contrast and viewpoint. The keep and tithe barn (now called the 'Archivbau') are impressive for their late Romanesque rustic ashlar masonry from the original building work around 1200. After the Upper Franconian Walpote family that lived here became extinct, the castle passed into the hands of the Hohenzollerns. Margrave Frederick had it restored while laying out Sanspareil Park. When you visit it, the unique panoramic view from the keep over the wooded hills of 'Franconian Switzerland' should certainly not be missed.

Top left: The Ruined Theatre in the Rock Garden of Sanspareil, made of undressed local tufa.

Top right: The Oriental Building is the centrepiece of a group of small park buildings.

Zwernitz Castle viewed from the south-east, where the Rock Garden of Sanspareil begins.

Stucco putti on the ceiling of the Great Hall.

Both from the outside and perhaps inside as well, the New Palace may seem to many visitors rather modest. Indeed, it cannot vie with palaces such as the Residence in Würzburg in size or splendour. And yet the Bayreuth house is considered to be among the masterpieces of 18th-century German architecture. The charm of the building lies not in grandiose, imposing architecture but in all the characteristics that go into the concept of Bayreuth Rococo—delicacy, refinement and intimacy of design. There is no artistic landscape in Germany like it.

The margravial couple Frederick and Wilhelmina had long harboured a wish to build a new palace from scratch. The Old City Palace, a remarkable Baroque building of the 17th century, met neither the loftier requirements of an absolutist court nor the greater demand for 18th-century comfort, as fashion from France decreed. The princely couple were finally forced to act when a fire on 26 January 1753 reduced the Old Palace largely to rubble and ashes. 'I allowed myself the pleasure of designing my palace myself', wrote Wilhelmina in a letter to her brother Frederick the Great. Though one need not take these words too literally, it is clear that the margravine had a major part in planning

The ceiling above one of the palace's two stairwells. The centrepiece of the ceiling stuccowork is a sunburst with putti, symbolizing Apollo. Margrave Frederick often identified himself with the Greek god.

and constructing the New Palace. The actual architectural design was supplied by Bayreuth court architect Joseph Saint-Pierre. Saint-Pierre had already built a number of residences and a church along the former riding arena and racecourse, thus creating a regular architectural ensemble, the later Schlossplatz in Ludwigstrasse. Margrave Frederick decided that these buildings should be bought and demanded that 'as many as possible be worked into the structure of the new palace'. Reconstructing the building history of the New Palace in detail is not a straightforward matter, since it proved possible for many parts of it, i.e. the already existing buildings, to be furnished and occupied after a short period of rebuilding even while building work was still in full swing elsewhere. The New Palace was basically complete by the time Wilhelmina died, in 1758, except for the little Italian House that Frederick built for his second wife (from 1759).

Let us visualize the result of the joint design work by Wilhelmina and Saint-Pierre in a tour through the palace. To reach the main entrance we shall first pass through the forecourt. At the back on either side is a **stairwell**, which leads from the relatively dark lower storey to the brightly lit upper storey, on whose ceiling a plaster sunburst sends forth its rays. This small architectural scene-setter is meant to indicate that the margrave's sphere is no longer entirely terrestrial, but lies somewhere between heaven and earth—corresponding to the image of the ruler as an intermediary between God and man, a notion that prevailed into the absolutist period. The first room we enter is the **Cavalry Guards' Room**, which was used by the royal couple's bodyguards. The room's function is evident from the filigree plasterwork with military emblems by Adam Rudolph Albini.

This sequence of rooms—the entrance, stairwell and guards' room—culminates in both size and grandeur in the next room, the **Great Hall.** Built to a square ground plan, it rises to the full height of the two upper storeys. The importance of the room is underlined by the majestic pilaster articulation. North and south of it are the wings of the margravine and margrave respectively.

After three large state rooms in the Ladies' Wing, altered in the 19th century, we enter the **Mirror Shard Room**, where only the ceiling is decorated.

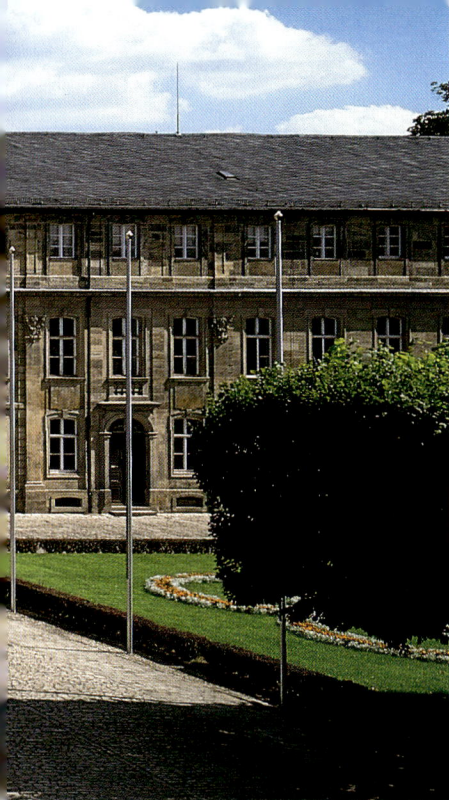

The New Palace with the Margrave's Fountain in front. The symmetrical design with the projecting central pavilion is, like the Opera House, based on French models.

Below: The Great Hall, which occupies the entire area of the central pavilion.

The Mirror Shard Room adjoins the official state apartments.

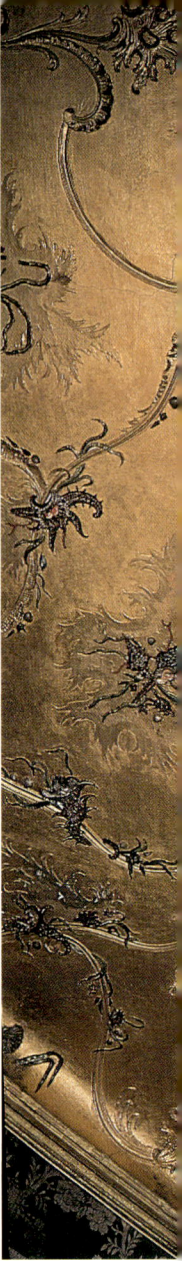

Arranged into curious 'Chinese' shapes, the shards surround a stuccoed centre scene showing a Chinese woman drinking tea. This is Margravine Wilhelmina herself, to whom a servant is submitting old Chinese scripts. As with the concepts that Wilhelmina sought to put across in the décor of her rooms in the Old Palace at the Hermitage, she has herself depicted here as a wise woman familiar with the philosophical writings of China.

Following the **Drawing Room with the gold ceiling**, this suite of rooms ends with the **Japanese Room**. Once again, the margravine was able to admire herself on the ceiling—this time as a sleeping Chinese woman. She is shown seated on a shell throne holding a pomegranate and a sprig of mustard in her hands. Because of their numerous seeds, both are symbols of life and fertility. Also remarkable is the wall decoration featuring exotic flower tendrils and brightly coloured Asiatic birds nestling among them. An additional fantastic effect is achieved by underpainting—the plaster was initially silvered over so as to give the subsequent paint layer a special sheen. The flower trellises suggest that, like the Chinese woman sleeping beneath the palm tree, we are outside in the fresh air.

Finally, we have yet to visit the **Old Music Room** in this part of the building. As in the Music Room at the Hermitage, the ceiling is adorned with a fresco of Orpheus. He has Wilhelmina's lapdog Folichon as a companion. Since

Detail of the wall decorations in the Japanese Room. Stucco ornament with exotic plants and birds.

The unusual motifs of shells and other marine creatures adorn the gold ceiling of the Drawing Room.

the margravine was passionately fond of music, this must have been one of her favourite rooms. Particularly notable are the pastel portraits of singers, musicians, dancers and actors integrated into the wall decoration. Some of these were done by Swedish painter Alexander Roslin, who was active in Bayreuth for a while before moving on to Paris to become one of the leading European portrait painters of the Enlightenment. A few of the pictures were probably painted by Wilhelmina herself.

The Margrave's Wing likewise has a number of splendid rooms, but these do not reflect the personality and ideas of their occupant in the way that Wilhelmina's do. We shall there-

Right: The light, cheerful walls of the Japanese Room are crowded with exotic birds of paradise between trellises surrounded by cacao palms and cacti.

An addition to the New Palace, the Italian House was built by Margrave Frederick in 1759 for his second wife, Sophia Caroline of Brunswick-Wolfenbüttel.

fore only visit the **Palm Room**, which is for many people the most enchanting room in the entire palace. As in the foregoing rooms, owing to the trellises, we seem to find ourselves out in the open once again. Carved, gilt palm branches are placed on strongly grained walnut panelling, their crowns reaching up to the sky, where dragons are seen in flight. Guests sitting down to a banquet here must have felt they were sitting in a palm grove.

Visitors in the 18th century were no doubt aware that, like virtually all decorative motifs in the New Palace, palms had multiple symbolic meanings. Palms, like cedars, are evergreens, and are therefore often an allusion to eternity. Moreover, their timber, leaves and fruits are all useful to man. Palm trees are therefore a symbol of life. Moreover the dragons in the picture, as Chinese symbols, stood for watchfulness. Therefore the decorative programme of the Palm Room implies that, in the margrave's realm, the population would be taken care

One of the console tables in the Palm Room modelled on laurel trees, which in the conceptual world of the Rococo symbolize peace.

Exotic natural motifs frequently reccur in the decorative programme of the Margravine's Apartments, and reappear here in Margrave Frederick's Palm Room.

of for eternity, in accordance with the qualities of the palm, while the ruler, in the form of dragons, keeps his vigilant eye on everything.

Besides the public rooms on the *piano nobile*, the ground floor of the **Italian House** also has impressive rooms. This building is a later addition that Margrave Frederick started for his second wife, Sophia Caroline of Brunswick-Wolfenbüttel in 1759, a mere year after the death of Wilhelmina. Here again Bayreuth Rococo, with its predilection for flower tendrils, trellis rooms and grottoes, comes into its own, though in a somewhat brittle, late form.

The showpiece rooms we have visited are of course the principal attractions of the New Palace. However, you should at all events pay a visit to the extensive Rummel Collection on the ground floor. This provides a complete overview of the artistic output of the former Bayreuth faïenceware manufactory. The displays about the work of theatre architect Galli Bibiena and the Bayreuth of Margravine Wilhelmina are also worth visiting. Finally, reference should likewise be made to a branch of the Bavarian State Painting Collections and the Archaeological Museum of the Upper Franconian Historical Association.

Summing up, one might say that 18th-century Bayreuth with its delightful houses and parks is largely the work of Wilhelmina—and that the town was an Arcadia dedicated to the enjoyment of life and a commentary in architecture, 41

The garden front of Fantaisie Palace. In the foreground is one of the sculptures in the 18th-century garden, a copy of a classical statue of the goddess of hunting, Artemis of Ephesus.

stucco and painting on the margravine as a person, a personality and woman of strong artistic preferences. It is quite simply astonishing what this petite, energetic woman managed to dream up and create in the over two decades between 1735 and 1758.

Fantaisie Palace and Park, Donndorf

The death of Wilhelmina did not put an end to building activity in margravial Bayreuth. Not only was the Italian House added to the New Palace, but a further important project was embarked on outside the town walls. This was the erection of an additional house and park, in Donndorf, just a few miles south-west of Bayreuth. The circumstances that fired renewed building ambitions in the margravial breast were twofold: in 1757, a fief had come back into Frederick's possession. It consisted of an extensive estate on which the lords of Lüchau had built a small castle in the 16th century. Moreover the margravial couple were still full of enthusiasm from their nearly year-long sojourn in Italy. One can easily imagine that Wilhelmina and her husband now wanted to build a house that should look more classical and also be rather grander than the Hermitage, which was really more of a *plaisance* than a respectable summer *Residenz*.

Wilhelmina did not live to see work start. Her constitution had always been fragile, and the exertions of the long journey resulted in her early demise at only 49. When Frederick commenced with the building in 1761, he wished to erect a separate, modern summer residence for his second wife. Yet he was not to see its completion either. Thus in 1763, Princess Frederica, inherited the estate and completed the house, to which she gave the richly ambiguous name Fantaisie. Following the failure of her marriage to Duke Charles Eugene of Württemberg, she had returned to Bayreuth, where she was to spend the rest of her life.

What the **palace** looked like, as a revival of the Bayreuth's golden age, we do not know, as later reconstruction work has left few traces of the period. Only a number of garden sculptures, the cascade and an elegant garden pavilion have survived. Many other things have since then been redesigned, such as a topiary garden and the legendary 'Spindler Room', whose walls and floor are entirely covered with precious wood inlays.

Today, the **park** is captivating for its staffage from the age of sentimentality and romanticism, when Fantaisie was in the possession of Princess Frederica and her son, Frederick. There is, for example, a replica of an Early Christian catacomb hewn out of rock, a Concord Column, St Alexander's Chapel and numerous secluded, restful seats.

In 2000, Germany's first garden museum was founded at Fantaisie, illustrating the history of landscape gardens from the 17th to the 19th century. It also pays homage to the time when some of the most original parks in Franconia—in fact, all Germany—came into being under Wilhelmina and Frederick.

The whole ground floor of the north-east wing of Ansbach's Residence is occupied by a huge, 150-foot-long room spanned by reticulated Gothic rib vaulting. Since 1971/72, this room has housed a collection of Ansbach faïence and porcelain.

ANSBACH

Residence

The small town of Ansbach had been incorporated into the Hohenzollern territories by purchase in 1331. Therewith Burgrave Frederick IV took a key step to round off his realm. As the position of the burgraves in Nuremberg became ever more precarious, finally leading to the destruction of the burgravial castle and sale of it to the city of Nuremberg in 1427, Burgrave Frederick VI had begun to focus more on his own territories. These were the circumstances that led to the construction of a moated castle in Ansbach in 1400. That this was an impressive structure is evident from the surviving rib vaulting in the rear wing of the Residence.

Frederick's son Albert Achilles succeeding in gaining control of the whole town, so that in 1456 he was able to move his principal seat from Cadolzburg to Ansbach. His grandson George the Pious followed contemporary fashion and had a **Gothic Hall** built, roofed throughout with reticulated vaulting. Some 150 feet long, it is one of the most magnificent halls of the period. The Residence had by then already reached roughly its present dimensions, though it acquired its current appearance from rebuilding in the Renaissance and subsequent work in the first half of the 18th century. The result is an outstanding example of German absolutist architecture, which involved architects Gabriel de Gabrieli, Karl Friedrich von Zocha and Leopold Retti.

Many people have scratched their heads trying to explain the unusual design of the façade. Two storeys high, with a rusticated ground floor, it is virtually unarticulated. It extends the length of 21 window bays without any

The arcaded courtyard was designed by Gabriel de Gabrieli and completed in 1738 by Leopold Retti.

The Great Hall of the Residence, with its musicians' gallery. Below the gallery are serving hatches to enable drinks to be served in the Great Hall.

One of four large reliefs of fine interior stuccowork by Diego Carlone above the doors of the Great Hall.

The ceiling painting in the Great Hall by Carlo Carlone dates from 1734. It glorifies the good government of Margrave Charles William Frederick (reg. 1729–57).

The Margrave's state bed and bedroom.

pavilion or temple feature to break the building line, except in two places where the wall projects forward an inch or two. Presumably, at Margrave Charles William Frederick's behest, Retti based his design on the garden front of Louis XIV's Versailles, the Sun King being the model for the Ansbach margrave in every respect. In the interiors of his palace, the margrave endeavoured to create grandeur in every conceivable way. Though this overstretched the financial capacity of the small margravate, it was not a matter for debate.

That in particular the stairwell did not end up more elaborate had nothing to do with thrift but with the presence of an existing structure, a Gothic castle dating from around 1400. Elsewhere, Retti was largely allowed free rein on the *piano nobile*, and could follow his artistic impulses unchecked. As no one room yields to any other in sumptuousness and the original building was preserved in its entirety, in our tour we can linger only in the most notable rooms.

The unsuspecting visitor of the time entered via the relatively steep staircase and almost plain **Guard Room**, only to be suddenly confronted with unexpected spaciousness and elegance as he entered the **Great Hall**. Once he reached the middle of the room, the layout became clear. Up in the musicians' gallery on the entrance wall, court musicians welcomed the guest with kettledrums and trumpets, while from a concealed serving hatch—a kind of bar, in fact—refreshments were served. The visitor's gaze would take in the marbled walls in the French style into which—as in the recesses—plaster reliefs by Diego Carlone are inserted. The painting overhead, covering the entire ceiling, was executed over a remarkably short period (May–December 1734) by his brother Carlo Carlone, one of the most successful fresco painters of the day.

A gilt chair in the Audience Chamber, 1740.

In the centre of the picture is an enthroned commander in Roman dress. This is not the margrave but an allegorical figure of the 'good ruler', who—almost literally in this case—floats in the sky above the palace. The monogram of the margrave appears in a cartouche. The allegorical figure is surrounded by the virtues Fortitude, Prudence and Justice, which the prince 'makes use of to leave his descendants immortal fame by his wise government', as an old description has it. The ideal ruler selected this place to sojourn because in Ansbach—so the picture implies—the same virtues are at home as form the company of 'good rulers' in heaven. This is how the allegory lauds the margrave, depicting him taking inspiration by gazing heavenwards, towards the ideal ruler. The scene can be interpreted as legitimizing the ruler. It is the quality of virtue invested in him by God that sets him apart from other people and predestines him for the role of ruler from birth. That the particular case of Charles William Frederick manifested a particularly dark reverse side of the medallion is another matter.

The next part of the tour of the palace takes us into the **Margrave's State Apartments**. Following ceremonial practice, two antechambers lead on to the margrave's **Audience Room**, containing the margrave's throne beneath a canopy. The stuccowork from the original building of 1737/40, like the decorations in the following **Bedroom**, goes back to similar work found in Versailles. This is principally remarkable in that nearby Bayreuth, which had family ties with Ansbach (the respective margraves were closely related and their wives were sisters), was culturally completely differently oriented, looking to Frederick the Great's Berlin for inspiration.

The principal bedroom betrays a personal touch with its many allusions to heron hawking and falconry. Charles William Frederick was devoted to field sports and reportedly slew 30,000 head of game in his lifetime. That did not mean the bedroom was really private, however. Field sports—particularly falconry—were traditional ruler attributes.

The next two rooms are of exceptional artistic quality and form a dazzling conclusion to the sequence of margravial rooms. Their very intimacy merely adds to the sense of progressive artistic merit. The **Brown Room**, which acted as the margrave's library, is notable for its richly carved wall panelling, while the following **Marble Room** derives its name from walls finished in marbled stucco. Set in the walls are allegorical paintings by Johann Adolf Biarelle alluding to the margrave.

Top left: The Brown Room was used by the Margrave as a reference library. The bookshelves are hidden behind oak panelling

Top right: The Hunting Room, the first antechamber of Margravine Frederica Louisa of Ansbach-Brandenburg (1714–1784), sister of Frederick the Great and Margravine Wilhelmina of Bayreuth.

Right: The extravagant stuccowork in the Mirror Room forms the *pièce de résistance* of the Margrave's Apartments.

Painting dating from *c.* 1740 by Johann Adolf Biarelle in Margrave Charles William Frederick's Marble Room.

Above left: The late Rococo gallery with its restrained ceiling stuccowork dates from 1771.

The **Margravine's Apartments** follow on directly from those of the margrave, though the first room we enter is in fact the last in the sequence, the principal access to her side being in the north-west wing, i.e. at the rear of the palace. This is a conspicuous break with tradition, since normally the two sets of apartments are mirror images of each other, on either side of a great hall. When you enter the margravine's quarters from the arcade walk in the courtyard, the grand overture of a great hall may be absent, but otherwise her rooms are in no way inferior to those of the margrave. The furnishings of the three antechambers become steadily more opulent towards the **Audience Room**, which is little different from the margrave's. The next room is a **Function Room**, whose splendid wooden panelling again recalls French models. Before reaching the **Bedroom**, the last room in the sequence, we enter the magnificent **Mirror Room**. As the name suggests, its walls are largely covered with mirrors, whereby the impression of an irrational dream world is multiplied a thousandfold. Countless porcelain figures, mainly Meissen, underline the special character of the room.

Like many other great houses of the time, such as Versailles or Schleissheim or even Bayreuth, the Ansbach palace has a **gallery**, though it was added later on. As far as court ceremonial is concerned, its importance lies in its position directly beside the Great Hall. It was a convivial room to receive company, where food could also be served. The **'Ordinary Dining Room'**, where meals were taken on less formal occasions, is separated from it by a small antechamber. Its notable feature is the wall decoration of 2,800 painted ceramic tiles made by an Ansbach manufactory. Attached to this is a third set of apartments, for guests. As in the case of the margravine's quarters, their position here on the *piano nobile* is unusual, and probably does not recur in any other great house.

Ornate cradle dating from before 1712, decorated with tortoiseshell and engraved pewter inlays.

2,800 tiles from the Ansbach tile manufactory give the 'Ordinary Dining Room' a pleasant, rustic character.

Perhaps better than any art-historical comparison, a remark by the proverbially thrifty Frederick the Great highlights the uncalled-for ostentation that no way matched Ansbach's economic situation. Once on a visit he is supposed to have asked his brother-in-law Charles William Frederick unsympathetically whether he imagined he was the Sun King.

Like so much in the Ansbach palace, the position of the park—the **Court Garden**—is likewise unusual owing to the existence of predecessors. It is not oriented to the palace as its main point of reference, as otherwise would be the case, but lies east of it on the other side of a road. Every symmetrical axial relationship—otherwise considered symbolically vital, particularly in the absolutist period—is absent. Around 1800 the grounds underwent major alterations, being transformed into a landscape garden, but the original Baroque structure can still be made out. It is basically crossed by two axes that intersect at the centre. The trees at the side have now grown into an impressive yet nonetheless quite unintended vault of lime trees. To offset the defective orientation in line with Baroque expectations, work was begun on an orangery at one end of an avenue in 1726. In its size and architectural pretensions—the north façade is a smaller version of the east façade of the Louvre—it almost achieves the grandeur of a full-scale great house itself.

EICHSTÄTT

The Renaissance-period Willibaldsburg Castle towers high above the River Altmühl.

Willibaldsburg Castle and Bastion Garden

The town looks back on a millennium and a quarter of history, to when Wessex-born Anglo-Saxon monk St Willibald became its first bishop, in 743. A further important date was 1305, when the bishops had to take the lead in preserving their rights and the security of the town, thereby taking over the function of rulers. Around this time, the Franconian Hohenzollerns had consolidated their fortunes and power. Following his acquisition of Ansbach, Frederick IV had considerably extended Zollern possessions. As a close confidant of Emperor Louis of Bavaria, he was able to secure numerous privileges for his family. Installing his two youngest sons on nearby episcopal thrones extended the Zollern sphere of influence still further: Frederick took over Regensburg and Berthold was appointed Bishop of Eichstätt by Pope Clement VI in 1351. Berthold likewise won the favour of the next emperor and acquired the influential post of chancellor (i.e. court secretary) to Charles IV. This secured him a visible position of power in the Holy Roman Empire, far beyond the borders of Franconia.

Directly after he was installed, Berthold embarked on the construction of a castle at Willibaldsburg, on a spur surrounded by the River Altmühl and overlooking the town. Even if this extension of power was short-lived, as Berthold occupied the see for only 11 years, the Zollerns could nonetheless show to all the world that with all their family links they were the leading ruling dynasty in Franconia.

From the Bastion Garden, the eye is drawn to the armoury and lateral wing of the castle.

Reconstruction of the *Hortus Eystettensis*, which in the early 17th century was one of the best-known gardens in Europe.

Coat of arms of Bishop Gabriel von Eyb, c. 1514, by Loy Hering.

During this period, i.e. the 14th century, the importance of the city of Eichstätt grew far beyond its function as an episcopal seat. Thus it was as much considerations of security as a desire to flaunt a highly visible symbol of secular power that prompted Berthold to move the bishop's residence from the city into the new fortified building. An ongoing construction programme subsequently enlarged it into an extensive complex of buildings, which in the early 17th century was expanded and rebuilt one final time to give the fortress its present appearance.

Rather comparably with Marienberg Fortress in Würzburg, the bastions of Willibaldsburg dominate the surrounding countryside. The main front is flanked by a pair of projecting corner towers. The architect of this proud building was Elias Holl from Augsburg, one of the leading exponents of the German Renaissance. The castle is still an impressive sight, even if the original design was only partly realized and the third storey and onion domes of the two towers were removed in the 19th century. The builder is thought to have been Bishop Johann Konrad von Gemmingen. His tomb in Eichstätt Cathedral shows him to have been a dignified, self-assured ruler. On his travels to England, France and Italy he acquired a patina of worldliness that is amply evident in the German late Renaissance style of Willibaldsburg.

After the prince-bishop's palace was removed back into the city in the 18th century, the fortress was subject to a long process of gradual decay, so that nowadays few original features in the interior survive. This is why the Jura Museum and Museum of Prehistory and Early History could be accommodated within it.

The **Bastion Garden**, reconstructed as recently as 1998, constitutes a particular attraction. It goes back to a once world-famous collection of plants that Bishop von Gemmingen took great pains to assemble. Proud of his work, he commissioned a series of engravings called the *Hortus Eystettensis*, featuring all 1,095 plants. The rarity and comprehensiveness of this collection is illustrated by the circumstance that only half the original stock of plants could be reassembled for the reconstruction of the *hortus*.

Residence of the Teutonic Order

Even before Berthold of Hohenzollern became Bishop of Eichstätt and laid the foundation stone for the Willibaldsburg, he already held high offices within the Teutonic Order. He had been admitted to the Order at the age of 13, and by 1345 had risen to the rank of provincial knight-commander—another example of the adroit tactical political skills of the Zollerns. At this date, the Order had still to acquire territorial independence, so its political influence was as yet limited.

It would be many turbulent centuries before Ellingen Palace, seat of the Franconian provincial commandery, finally achieved its present form. The medieval castle was followed initially by a Renaissance palace, rises were followed by falls. The Order—originally a religious organization with numerous charitable functions—had in the meantime largely become a worldly power with a matching love of ostentation, as was customary with all rulers in the absolutist age.

The present appearance of the palace's **New Building** was erected by provincial commander Charles Henry, Baron of Hornstein, immediately after

The Ellingen Residence is located on the edge of a village, in unspoilt countryside.

Above and below, right: The symmetrical exterior of the palace chapel conceals a Gothic chapel that later underwent a Baroque makeover.

being appointed in 1718. The architect he employed was Franz Keller. Starting from the predecessor buildings, he erected the house to enclose a courtyard. The south front is notable for its emphasized vertical features. The three prominent projections stand on high, rusticated plinths. Monumental pilasters likewise accentuate the façade's verticality. The whole majestic building has an effect of solidity and massiveness rather than breadth. The **chapel**, originally Gothic but later rebuilt in the Baroque style, occupies the whole length of the north front. An unusual feature in 18th-century houses, it is a reminder of the original religious nature of the Order. Apart from the sump-

Left: The palace has a magnificent Baroque stairwell.

tuous decoration of the chapel, the stuccoed decoration of this period is best preserved in the stairwell. As a theatrical flourish, the **stairwell** is a relatively early example of a whole series of other well-known examples in Franconia, the apogee being the magnificent stairwell in Würzburg. Part of the Baroque decoration in the **Royal Apartments** has also survived the ravages of time. The most impressive is probably the **Marquetry Room**, where the floor, the lower parts of the walls and window niches are covered with inlaid scenes based on engravings by Jacques Callot.

The rest of the interior was completely rebuilt from 1771, presumably after a fire, when the celebrated French architect Pierre-Michel d'Ixnard was summoned to redesign quite a number of rooms. Forty years later, when the Teutonic Order was abolished, the palace passed into the hands of Prince Charles Philip of Wrede, who had received it from the Bavarian king, Maximilian I, as a reward for his successful military contribution to Napoleon's downfall. With the completion of the furnishings, Ellingen became a prime example of the inroads made by Neoclassicist elegance into German great houses. Nowadays, visitors can also explore an exhibition on the Teutonic Knights as well as the historic rooms.

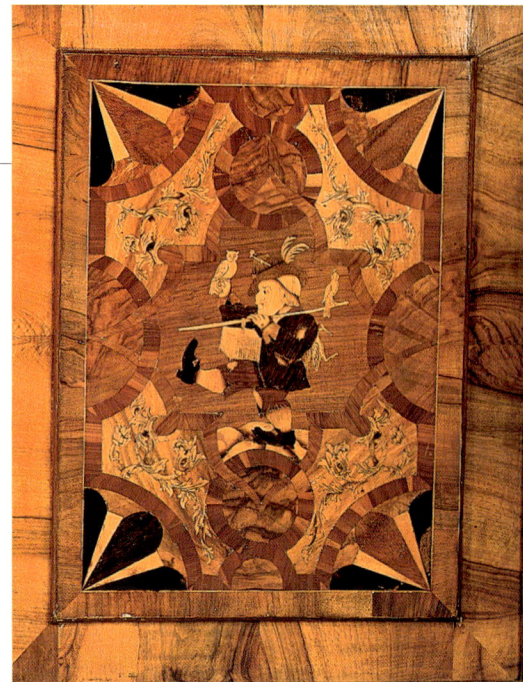

Around 1720, the floor and skirting boards of the Marquetry Room were decorated with precious inlays based on a series of engravings by Jacques Callot.

This classical-style chair was made c. 1770 in Ansbach or England.

COBURG

Coburg Castle

When Otto VIII, Duke of Merania and Count Palatinate of Burgundy, died without issue in 1248, it was the end of an era. Otto was the last in the line of the Bavarian Counts of Diessen and Andechs, who had meteorically risen to the rank of a European ruler. His immense possessions, which comprised Burgundy, Istria and parts of Franconia, including the domains of Plassenburg and Coburg, were divided up. Plassenburg went to the Counts of Orlamünde and the Hohenzollerns, Coburg to the Counts of Henneberg and thence to the Wettins. Two strong trunks developed from common roots, which grew separately into two of the most powerful ruling houses in the Holy Roman Empire. Their amicable relations stemmed not just from geographical proximity, but also from intermarriage—though of course this did not necessarily always produce a happy outcome, as the example of the last Ansbach margrave Alexander and Princess Frederica of Saxe-Coburg showed.

Begun long before the change of power, Coburg Castle was first mentioned in 1056. The handover to the Wettins came in 1353, and thereafter its strategic importance meant it was constantly being improved and became well-nigh impregnable, dominating the countryside for miles around. It is certainly one of the largest and finest strongholds in Germany.

Like many castles, the fortress consists of an outer (in parts triple) ring of curtain walls containing an **outer bailey** and within that the **castle proper**. The Late Gothic armoury (mid-15th century), also called the **Tall House**, is the best-preserved part of the stronghold. The castle itself on the eastern side consists mainly of the **Prince's Building**, behind the half-timbering of which the remains of the former *Palas* are hidden together with the **Ladies' Rooms** (*Hohe Kemenate*). Most impressive is

The promontory on which Coburg Castle was built in the 10th century has been inhabited since 2000 BC.

Clock tower and Ladies' Rooms at Coburg Castle.

the **Horn Room**, one of the finest marquetry rooms in Germany. Made in 1632 for Ehrenburg Palace, the wood inlays and carvings depict hunting scenes. The castle played an important part in the history of the Reformation by sheltering Martin Luther for a lengthy period. During the Diet at Augsburg, he worked on his translation of the Scriptures into German here.

That the fortress is so well preserved, even though it ceased to have any strategic value from the 18th century, was the merit of Duke Ernest I. In his romantic enthusiasm for the German Middle Ages, he not only prevented it from falling into total ruin but even got distinguished architect Carl Alexander von Heideloff to give it a work-over in Gothic Revival style, as a symbol of the venerability of his family.

Nowadays, the castle houses the former ducal art collections: a major collection of engravings, parts of the glass collection, the armoury and an outstanding collection of Old German paintings, to mention only a few of its treasures.

Portrait of Martin Luther, c. 1540, workshop of Cranach. Luther spent several months at Coburg Castle.

Scenes in the Horn Room are eloquent of the Coburg dukes' passion for hunting.

EHRENBURG PALACE

The Gothic Revival look of Ehrenburg Palace goes back to Karl Friedrich Schinkel's reconstruction of the Baroque palace.

Around the mid-16th century, Coburg underwent a profound change in cultural consciousness. With Duke John Ernest, the Renaissance reached a new staging post on its triumphal march through Europe. An external token thereof was moving the court from Coburg Castle into the town, where the duke had a new palace erected, first occupied in 1547.

Following a fire in 1690, work was begun on a Baroque-style palace. It consisted of a *corps de logis* with two wings at right angles to it. As these wings were as long as the main block in the middle, a very deep *cour d'honneur* was created. There is little here of the theatrical effect so typical of Baroque architecture, and that also applies to the asymmetrical, functional arrangement of the interior. The **state rooms** were accommodated in the main block, while the east wing was used for **guest apartments**. The west wing was reserved for the court **chapel** and **Great Hall** above. Both have retained their original appearance, but few other rooms survive from this first building period.

The palace was renovated and partly rebuilt in the decades after 1810, four years after Duke Ernest inherited the title. Duke Ernest was an outstanding personality who had drunk deep of the spirit of Romanticism. With an enthusiasm for medieval architecture and art, he did much rebuilding at Coburg Castle, at Rosenau Palace nearby and finally at Ehrenburg. He commissioned no lesser a figure than the young Berlin architect Karl Friedrich Schinkel to redesign the façade of the palace. It was wholly to the duke's taste—possibly

even requested by him—that Schinkel resorted to the English Gothic Revival for inspiration. It was a very daring decision, as the Gothic Revival had up to then not been used in any comparable building in Germany. With this redesign by Schinkel, the structure took on a whole new character. Whereas previously Ehrenburg had resembled a palace, it now looked more like an English country house.

The interior was similarly adapted to contemporary fashions, in several phases, as is evident on a tour through the building. The **stairwell** and adjacent **Antechamber** and **Family Room** were designed around 1830 by Gottlieb Eberhard in a historicist neo-Renaissance style. Turning westwards, one reaches the **Great Hall**, the most important and palatial room in the complex from the post-1690 building period. It is so original in conception that it is worth a close look.

Twenty-eight majestic atlantes are, as it were, heroic figures of antiquity in the ducal service, in a line along the walls. With their muscular nakedness and varying attitudes they look very alive. With one hand they hold lamps, while with the other they prop up the entablatures resting on their heads, or, if directly side by side, they embrace each other. Dramatic *stuccatura* by Carlo Domenico and Bartolomeo Lucchese with splendid garlands divides the ceiling into sections. At the sides, there are earthly scenes of the arts and sciences, while the centre fields display *trompe l'œil* palace and church architecture. In the centre is a dome with Minerva, goddess of the arts and sciences, in the middle looking as if she were passing by and just landed.

The neo-Renaissance stairwell is decorated with copies of classical statues.

Right: Twenty-eight massive atlantes are the dominant feature in the Baroque Great Hall, which was begun after 1690.

Portrait of Prince Albert of Saxe-Coburg Gotha (1819–1861), son of Duke Ernest, painted by Franz Xaver Winterhalter *c.* 1845. Prince Albert became the consort of Victoria, Queen of Great Britain and Ireland.

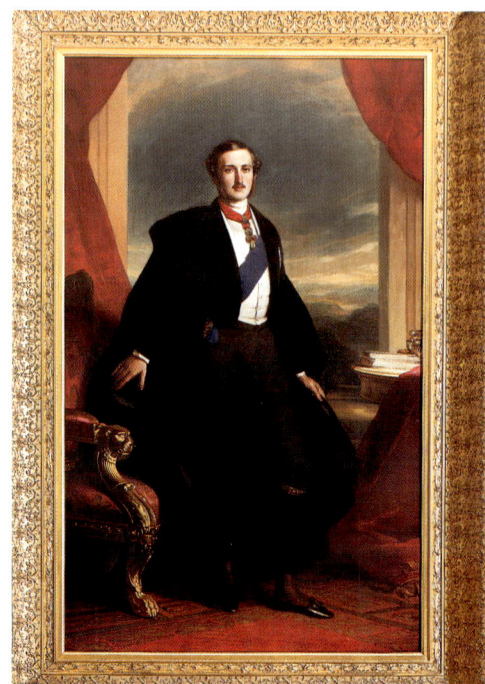

Portrait of Queen Victoria (1819–1901), likewise by Franz Xaver Winterhalter. Queen Victoria was Albert's cousin as well as his wife.

The reference is clearly to John Casimir, the highly cultured duke who was intellectually still thoroughly at home in the world of humanism. His enlightened rule had established an age of peace in the Coburg realms (their geographical extent is indicated by the 56 coats of arms in the recess)—an allusion to the duchy's recovery from the devastating consequences of the Thirty Years' War. A profusion of tendrils suggests that want had been banished from the land. An effect of times of peace is that the arts and sciences, encouraged and endorsed by the duke, are enthusiastically going about their work once more. Minerva has therefore come to visit this temple of peace to find a new home here. In a golden age of the kind the duke had in mind from his knowledge of classical mythology, life becomes one huge celebration. That in brief is the interpretation of the Coburg Great Hall.

In the east wing opposite the Great Hall is the **Throne Room**. Designed by Parisian architect André-Marie Renié-Grétry, it took around 15 years to build. Work on it and other rooms was funded by war reparations that France had to pay in 1815 after its defeat in the German Wars of Liberation. Even though Napoleon, who had been an ally until his defeat at the Battle of the Nations in Leipzig, was himself now under siege, Coburg stuck to Neoclassicism, which had gained favour Europe-wide under Napoleon's rule. In this, Coburg was no different from Munich.

Behind the Throne Room are further state rooms, including the **Audience Chamber** and Duke Ernest's **Study**. Of particular interest is the final room in the series, the **Bedroom**. In 1840, Prince Albert (born 1819), the duke's second son,

Between 1816 and 1833, Duke Ernest had the walls of the Baroque Throne Room refurbished in a heavy Neoclassical style.

Clock with putti blowing soap bubbles, in the study. Made in Paris *c.* 1815.

married his similarly aged cousin Victoria, the legendary British queen, after whom a whole era would be named. Whenever Victoria stayed in Coburg, she occupied this room. She brought with her the idea of the lavatory installed beside the bed, a full-scale water closet encased in mahogany. It was one of the first of its kind on the Continent.

The rooms of the storey below were occupied by Duchess Louisa of Saxe-Gotha-Altenburg, Ernest's first wife. These were also furnished in the Empire style, though as the **Ladies' Apartments** they were much more orna-mental. The decorative motifs are different on the two floors. Whereas the ducal rooms frequently feature heraldic and military motifs, the duchess's chambers tend to contain allusions to love and marriage. The two sets of apartments could thus be attributed to Mars, the god of war and patron of the state, and the love goddess Venus.

Finally we should take a look inside the **Court Chapel** built between 1690 and 1701. The first astonishing feature is its size. Two storeys high, it is a hall church occupying the entire length and breadth of the west wing. A second sur-prise is that it is a Protestant church, for there is no trace here of the modera-

In 1825, Duke Ernest had his study completely refurbished in the Empire style. The painting in the middle is by Ludwig Döll and shows Duchess Louisa (1800–1831), the duke's first wife, with her two children, Ernest and Albert, c. 1823/24.

Detail of the ceiling in the duchess's boudoir, painted in the early 19th century in a playful variant of the French Directoire style.

tion in decorative opulence associated with Lutheranism. Richly adorned with frescoes and stucco and containing a ciborium altar modelled on that in St Peter's in Rome, the church would have no trouble in being passed off as Catholic—except for two features: first, a pulpit rather than an altar painting is the focal point of the sanctuary and indeed the whole church, and secondly the subject of the extensive series of frescoes is the Revelation of St John the Divine, a rarely painted subject with its references to death and the end of the world. This sombre, apocalyptic subject matter does not seem compatible with the splendid world of absolutism and the glorification of power, especially if we compare it with the decorative schemes of other contemporary palace chapels, for example the one in Versailles built a little later. Both churches represent the two-storey palace chapel type, where the upper floor is reserved for the ruler. In both, the organ is even placed over the altar; despite the stylistic differences, both are sumptuously decorated— and both more or less occupy a whole wing of the building. Both share the delight in courtly splendour. But in the Sun King's palace chapel the ceiling fresco of the Resurrection of Christ stands for the triumph of the Church, whose earthly representative his 'Most Catholic Majesty' considered himself to be. In Versailles, this was the transfiguration of the festive moment, compared with the awareness of the frailness of all mortality in Coburg. Ultimately, the mentality of the French Catholic and the German Protestant— Duke Albert—could hardly have been more different.

Rosenau Palace and Park, Rödental

'If I were not what I am, this would be my real home.' This confession was written by no less a person than Queen Victoria. She was not speaking of a palace in her far-flung Empire but Rosenau Palace, by the River Itz in Rödental and only a few miles from Coburg. Her husband, Prince Albert, had been born here in 1819, the son of Duke Ernest who had Coburg Castle restored and Ehrenburg rebuilt in the Neoclassical style.

The new duke had hardly come into his title when work began on transforming the medieval castle in 1808. The result, an atmospheric Gothic Revival building set in an extensive landscape garden, was completed by 1817. Karl Friedrich Schinkel had also contributed plans for the duke's summer residence. The comfortable country house was furnished in the Biedermeier style. The walls are mostly painted, while the furniture was obtained in Vienna.

The building is entered via a Gothic hall, which is also called the **Marble Room** because of its wall cladding. Beside this is an octagonal **Library.** The tradition is that chivalric novels were collected here, and indeed, the paintings in some of the spaces enclosed within pointed arches show scenes of knights, based on a novel by Friedrich de la Motte Fouqué. The upper storey contained the ducal rooms, many of which have now been restored to their original appearance following expensive restoration work. Only in the case of what is arguably the most original room was reconstruction not possible owing to a lack of sufficient information. It was designed as a free-standing vine arbour with a view of 'the mountains of Helvetia'. If you looked out the window, of course, you did not actually see the Alps, but an extensive **landscape garden.** Even

Miniature copied from the painting *May Day 1851* by Franz Xaver Winterhalter. Depicted are Queen Victoria and Prince Albert with their seventh child, Prince Arthur, and the Duke of Wellington, who is presenting the prince with a gift.

Marble Room and ducal Drawing Room.

Top: Rosenau Palace, which was rebuilt by Duke Ernest from 1808 in a Gothic Revival style.

despite later changes, it still encompasses two lakes, a hermitage, a grotto and a Neoclassical orangery, which is now used to house a museum for modern glass.

How far the residents of Rosenau really took the medieval spirit can be deduced from the tournament that Duke Ernest organized to celebrate the completion of Rosenau. Medieval costume was also worn at festivities. In its return to a 'national' style—even if inspired by English example—Rosenau Palace is the clearest expression of Duke Ernest's Romantic enthusiasms.

63

Front cover: Sun Temple at the Hermitage in Bayreuth
Front flap: Carving in the auditorium of the Margravial Opera House in Bayreuth
Back flap: Mirror Room in the Ansbach Residence

© for text, design and layout by Prestel Verlag, Munich · Berlin · London · New York 2003

© for illustrations: All illustrations are from the archives of the Bavarian Administration of State Castles, Palaces, Gardens and Lakes (including C. Carretta, M. Custodis, K. Frahm, A. Lang, T. Mayr, L. Weiss) with the exception of p. 5: Staatsarchiv Nürnberg; p. 7 (bottom), p. 10 (bottom): Verlag Schnell & Steiner/ Roman von Götz, Regensburg; p. 13 (top): Herbert Liedl, Nuremberg; p. 13 (bottom left): Museen der Stadt Nürnberg, Museum Tucherschloss; p. 14 (top): Hans Werner Kress, Cadolzburg; p. 16 (top), p. 18 (top and bottom), pp. 26/27, p. 30: Feuerpfeil Verlag, Bayreuth; p. 17 (bottom): M. Zenkel, Ansichtskarten-verlag; p. 33 (top and bottom): Karl-Heinz Weisfloch, Kulmbach; p. 55 (top and bottom), p. 56 (top and bottom): Kunstsammlungen der Veste Coburg; p. 57(top): Staatsarchiv Coburg, Plansammlung; p. 57 (bottom): Feldrapp, Naila.

Cartography: Anneli Nau, Munich

Prestel Verlag, Königinstrasse 9, D-80539 Munich
Tel. +49 (89) 38 17 09-0, Fax +49 (89) 38 17 09-35

Prestel Publishing Ltd., 4, Bloomsbury Place, London WC1A 2QA
Tel. +44 (20) 7323-5004, Fax +44 (20) 7636-8004

Prestel Publishing, 175 Fifth Avenue, Suite 402, New York, N.Y. 10010
Tel. +1 (212) 995-2720, Fax +1 (212) 995-2733
www.prestel.com

The Library of Congress Cataloguing-in-Publication data is available.

Die Deutsche Bibliothek holds a record of this publication in the Deutsche Nationalbibliographie; detailed bibliographical data can be found under: http://dnb.dde.de

Prestel books are available worldwide. Please contact your nearest bookseller or one of the above addresses for information concerning your local distributor.

Translated from the German by Paul Aston, Dorset, England
Edited by Michele Schons, Munich
Designed and typeset by Norbert Dinkel, Munich
Origination by Reproline, Munich
Printed and bound by Sellier Druck GmbH, Freising

ISBN 3-7913-2642-2 (English edition)
ISBN 3-7913-2641-4 (German edition)